D1219272

BUILDINGS AT WORK

Airports

ELIZABETH ENCARNACION

QEB Publishing

Library of Congress Control Number: 2006038434

ISBN 978 1 59566 374 0

Written by Elizabeth Encarnacion
Designed by Rahul Dhiman (Q2A Media)
Series Editor Honor Head
Foldout illustration by Ian Naylor
Picture Researcher Sujatha Menon

Publisher Steve Evans
Creative Director Zeta Davies
Senior Editor Hannah Ray

Printed and bound in China

CONTENTS

AIRPORTS

Airports are found all over the world. People going away on vacation or on business trips use airplanes to fly them between both international and **regional airports**. Some people have their own private airplanes that they keep in smaller airports. Fighter jet pilots take off from military air bases to fly missions or go on practice flights. Medical teams land helicopters on hospital **helipads**, so their patients can be treated faster. Airports serve many different purposes, but they all have a few basic things in common, such as a place to take off and land, areas for parking the planes, and an **air traffic controller** or equipment to help the pilot land.

FACT!

The King Fahd International Airport in Saudi Arabia is bigger than the entire country of Bahrain! It is 301 square miles (780 square kilometres) and is the world's largest airport in size.

Island hopping

Hong Kong International Airport is an engineering wonder built on a man-made island. It has the world's largest airport **terminal**, a huge space for handling **cargo**, and two **runways** that deal with about 750 airplanes per day. It is the fifth busiest airport in the world. The world's longest **suspension bridge** was built to connect the airport to the city of Hong Kong. The bridge is 4,518 feet (1,377 meters) long and both cars and trains travel across it.

▲ More than 40 million people travel through Hong Kong International Airport every year.

▲ Gigantic double-decker airplanes, such as the new Airbus A380, can carry up to 555 passengers.

◀ An airport's air ▶ traffic controllers work together with the terminal staff and ground crew to keep passengers and planes moving.

SUPER PLANES

Enormous double-decker airplanes such as the Airbus A380 are being ordered by airlines to transport large numbers of people over long distances. They are also used by courier companies for delivering goods. These huge aircraft need longer and wider runways, so many airports will have to be redesigned. Runways may have to be widened and terminal gates replaced because of the size of these planes.

INTERNATIONAL AIRPORTS

International airports are the largest and busiest type of airport. Hundreds of flights a day land and take off on their runways, and thousands of passengers pass through their terminals. International airports are so busy because they are both a **destination** and a **transfer point** to other cities. If there is not a direct flight from a passenger's local airport to their destination, they can fly to an international airport and then catch a plane that flies where they want to go.

THE WORLD'S BUSIEST

For almost a decade, Hartsfield-Jackson Atlanta International Airport in Georgia has been the world's busiest airport. The amount of traffic at an airport can be figured out in two ways: by totaling the number of airplanes that take off or land or by counting the number of passengers who fly in or out, or transfer through the airport. Atlanta is currently first in both categories because almost a million planes and nearly 86 million passengers use the airport each year.

▲ The Hartsfield-Jackson Atlanta International Airport employs 55,300 people.

Foreign visitors

At all international airports, passengers flying in from a foreign country have to go through immigration and customs. An immigration agent checks each passenger's passport and may stamp it with the date and country of arrival. Some countries have computers that can **scan** passports to make sure the passenger is entering the country legally, while other airports have video cameras with computers that can recognize people who may be traveling in disguise. After the passengers have collected their bags, they go through customs. Passengers have to tell the customs officials about any unusual items they are carrying, such as food that might carry diseases or goods that are over a certain value. These goods might be **confiscated** or the passenger may have to pay to bring them into the country.

▲ Passengers traveling from other countries must show their passports at immigration.

▲ International airports have several terminals and a large system of runways and **taxiways**.

7

REGIONAL AIRPORTS

Regional airports are found in smaller cities and do not usually offer international flights—the planes at these airports generally only fly to or from other cities inside their own country. Some of the flights from a regional airport offer **connections** to an international airport. Passengers from different places can fly to the regional airport first in a small aircraft, then share one larger plane to the international airport. This helps to reduce the traffic at the larger airports.

▲ Smaller passenger planes, such as this one in Dallas, Texas, provide regular flights from one part of the same country to another.

On the ground

At both regional and international airports, when an airplane is parked at the terminal between trips, a **ground crew** prepares it for the next flight. Baggage handlers open the **hold** of the plane and unload the luggage onto carts. Other workers refuel the plane with jet fuel and check the outside of the plane for any problems. A cleaning crew boards the plane to tidy up after the previous flight while a catering company refills the food supplies in the onboard kitchens.

8

CARRYING CARGO

Bigger airports usually have special cargo planes that carry anything from small cardboard boxes to giant metal containers. Smaller boxes that are traveling to the same destination are wrapped together to make them easier to load into the plane. Cargo planes have the same basic structure as passenger planes, but they have a flat, open area where containers can be strapped down instead of rows of seats. Some cargo planes have only one large cargo area to take very big containers. Many passenger planes carry cargo in their baggage holds for a fee.

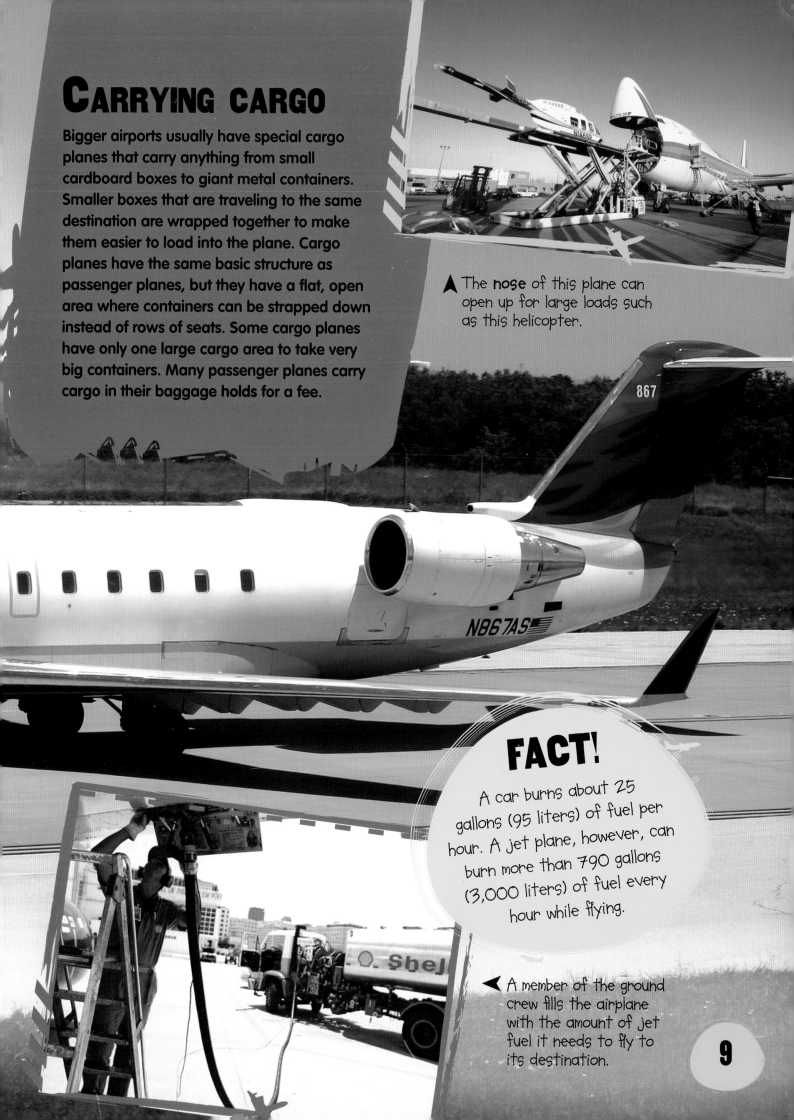

▲ The **nose** of this plane can open up for large loads such as this helicopter.

FACT!

A car burns about 25 gallons (95 liters) of fuel per hour. A jet plane, however, can burn more than 790 gallons (3,000 liters) of fuel every hour while flying.

◄ A member of the ground crew fills the airplane with the amount of jet fuel it needs to fly to its destination.

9

TERMINAL

Airport terminals are buildings in which passengers buy tickets, **check in** their luggage, go through security checks, and wait for their flights. Terminals often have stores and restaurants to help people pass the time. Most international airports have more than one terminal. The terminals are joined by walkways, buses, or trains. Each terminal has many **gates** where passengers get on or off the airplanes.

Baggage handling

When a passenger checks in at the ticket counter, an airline agent attaches a tag with a unique **barcode** to each bag that is going into the hold. The bags are placed on a **conveyor belt** and screened by security staff, who X-ray the bags and check them for dangerous materials. The barcode on each piece of luggage is then scanned to find out where the bag should go, and the luggage is carried by another conveyor belt to the correct baggage cart. Baggage handlers drive the cart to the right airplane and load the bags.

▼ Passengers show their tickets and passports to a member of airline staff when they check in.

KEEPING THE SKIES SAFE

All passengers must go through security screening in the terminal before they are allowed to board a plane. Any bags passengers want to carry with them onto the plane must go through an X-ray machine so that security guards can look for any sharp items, such as scissors and penknives. The passenger then walks through a large metal detector. If the detector buzzes, a security guard will wave a smaller, handheld detector over the passenger to find the exact source of the metal and check that it is nothing dangerous. A new machine called an explosive trace portal is also sometimes used during security screening. It is nicknamed "puffer" because it blows little puffs of air that knock loose small particles on a person's skin, hair, and clothes. The machine then studies these particles for tiny amounts of explosive chemicals that anyone who had been in contact with these materials would have on their body.

▲ X-ray machines allow security staff to see what is inside passengers' bags without having to open and search through each one.

▼ Air terminals are designed to make passengers feel comfortable and find their airplanes easily.

FACT!

The Hajj Terminal at King Abdul Aziz International Airport in Jeddah, Saudi Arabia, is used for only a few days each year, when thousands of Muslims from around the world travel to Mecca as part of their religion. The terminal can hold as many as 80,000 people under its tent-shaped roof.

AIRFIELD

The airfield is the part of the airport where the planes move around. Planes take off and land on the long, straight runways. Taxiways are roads near the runways that pilots use to move airplanes from one place to another. There are colored lights on the runways and taxiways so that pilots can find their way around at night. The area outside the terminal where the planes park is called the ramp and is also part of the airfield.

Many airports have more than one runway that face in different directions. This is so that planes can take off into the wind, no matter which direction the wind is blowing.

Marking the spot

Runways and taxiways are painted with lines and numbers so that pilots can tell them apart. A taxiway is usually narrower than a runway and has a solid yellow line down the center. The edges of a runway are marked with two white lines, and a dotted white line runs down the middle. Eight white stripes above a giant number mark the beginning of a runway. Different combinations of white stripes let the pilots know how far they are from the **touchdown** area during landings.

FIX IT

When part of an airplane needs to be repaired, the plane is taken to a maintenance hangar. This is a huge building that can hold several planes at a time and has a large door that can close to protect the planes from the weather. In the hangar, workers can build scaffolding around the aircraft, and take large sections of the plane apart to replace faulty parts.

▼ A jet engine is repaired in the maintenance hangar.

Taxiway

FACT!

Every runway is different, but an average runway at a major airport is made of concrete about 3 feet (1 meter) thick and 9,843 feet (3,000 meters) long.

◄ Airplanes drive slowly down the taxiway to get to the runway, where they will speed up for takeoff.

13

SAFETY SYSTEMS

Air traffic controllers work in an air traffic control tower. This is a circular building that rises high above the airport and has huge glass windows all the way around. Air traffic controllers give the pilots information on weather conditions and how and where to land, so that they do not run into each other. Ground controllers direct the pilots as they drive down taxiways to get to and from the runway, while local controllers use binoculars and **radar** to tell pilots when and where to approach the airport for landing and how fast they should go during take off.

ON FIRE

Airports have their own fire stations near the runways, so fire engines can reach any plane that is on fire within minutes. An airport fire engine can carry and spray large amounts of water and foam to fight the extra-hot flames created by the jet fuel used by planes. The special fire engines also have more tires than a normal fire truck, so they can drive on a rougher surface if a plane has crashed off the runway.

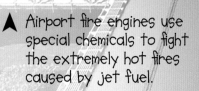

▲ Airport fire engines use special chemicals to fight the extremely hot fires caused by jet fuel.

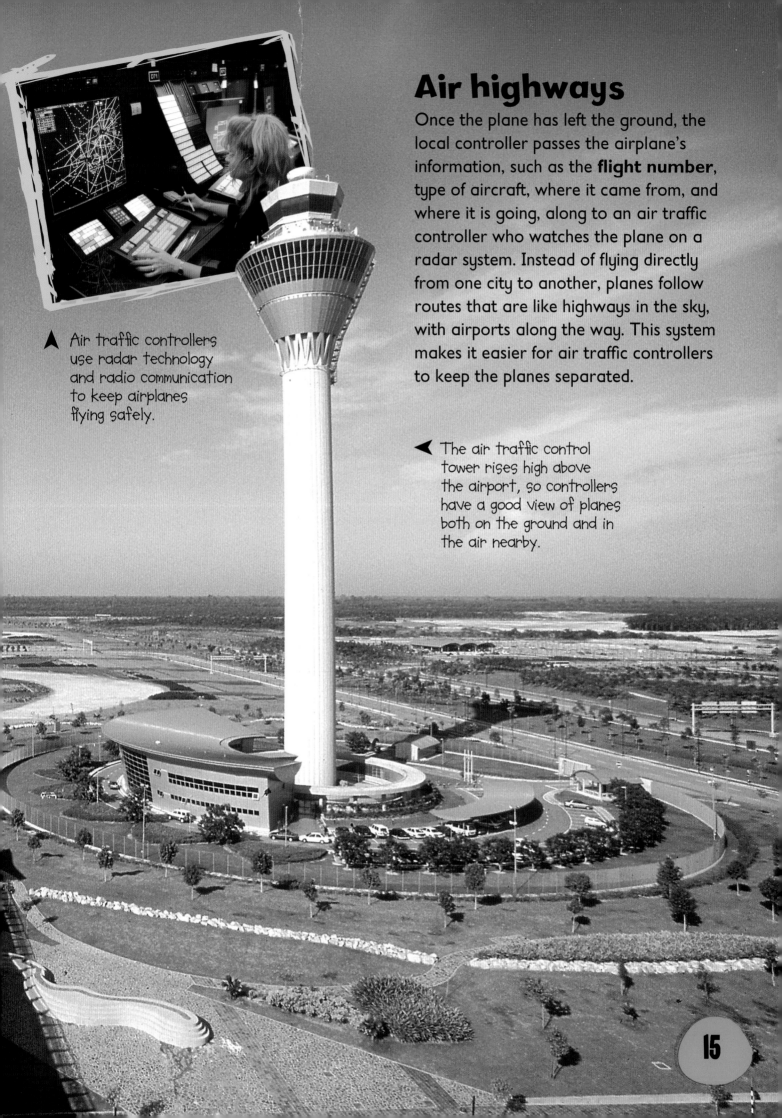

Air highways

Once the plane has left the ground, the local controller passes the airplane's information, such as the **flight number**, type of aircraft, where it came from, and where it is going, along to an air traffic controller who watches the plane on a radar system. Instead of flying directly from one city to another, planes follow routes that are like highways in the sky, with airports along the way. This system makes it easier for air traffic controllers to keep the planes separated.

◄ Air traffic controllers use radar technology and radio communication to keep airplanes flying safely.

◄ The air traffic control tower rises high above the airport, so controllers have a good view of planes both on the ground and in the air nearby.

15

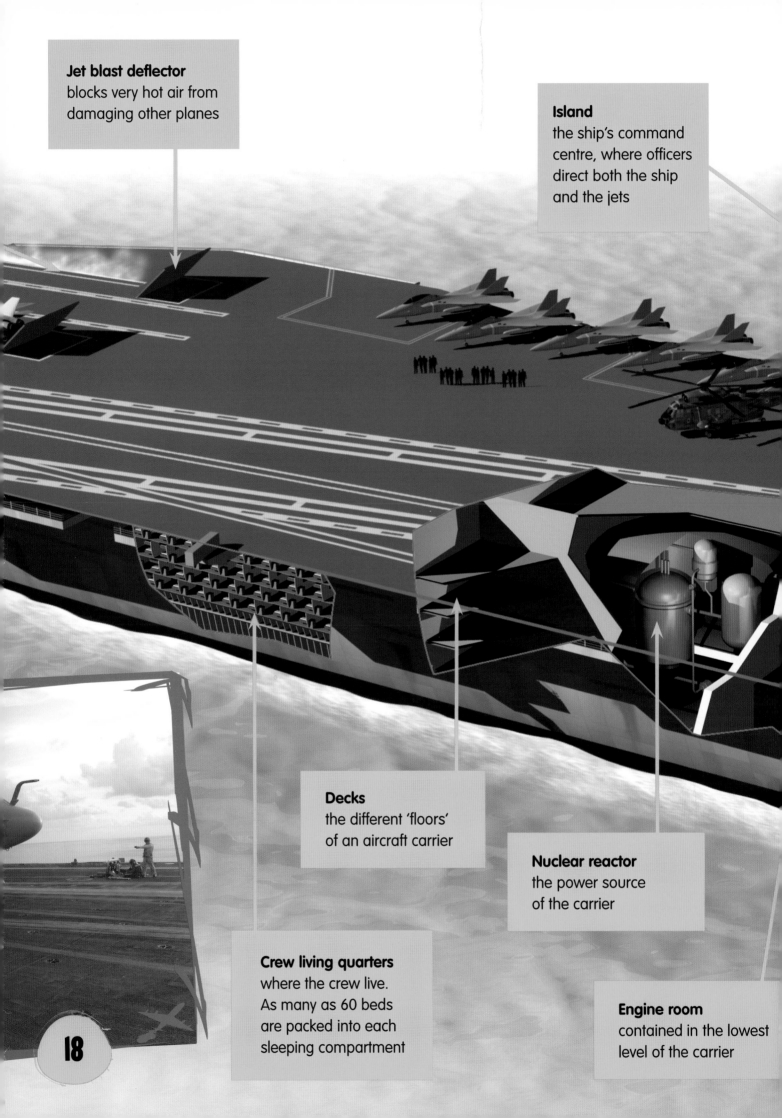

Jet blast deflector
blocks very hot air from damaging other planes

Island
the ship's command centre, where officers direct both the ship and the jets

Decks
the different 'floors' of an aircraft carrier

Nuclear reactor
the power source of the carrier

Crew living quarters
where the crew live. As many as 60 beds are packed into each sleeping compartment

Engine room
contained in the lowest level of the carrier

18

Catapult
powered by steam.
Gives the jet planes
enough speed to
take off safely

flight deck
where the jets
take off and land

Taking off and landing

An aircraft carrier's flight deck is much
shorter than a typical runway, so the
planes need help to reach high speeds for
takeoff and to stop quickly when landing.
On most carriers, a member of the crew
connects the aeroplane's front wheel to a
catapult that uses steam power to fling
the plane down the runway at speeds of
up to 296 kilometers per hour so that it
can take off. When coming in to land,
the pilot will lower the plane's **tailhook**
and attempt to hook it on one of the four
arresting wires stretched across the
runway. Some aircraft carriers have a
runway that slopes up like a ski jump,
giving planes the lift needed for takeoff
and slowing them down during landing
without using catapults and arresting
cables.

➤ An EA-6B Prowler gets
ready to launch from
an aircraft carrier.

17

MILITARY AIR BASES

Military air bases have airfields with the same basic parts as **civilian** airfields: a runway, taxiways, ramps, and support buildings. However, they may also have storage areas for guns and missiles, large temporary parking areas for visiting aircraft, and open areas for flying training missions. Many **test flight**s are also held at air bases, where very experienced pilots try out new types of aircraft.

▼ Military airplanes often park in rows on the airfield, rather than at a passenger terminal.

Training

Learning to fly a military airplane can take several years of training. First, the new recruit must complete basic military training. Then he or she must learn to fly a small civilian plane. Once the pilot is qualified to fly, he or she is given a test to find out what type of aircraft they are best suited to—fighter jets, bombers, attack helicopters, or transport planes. Pilots then go through specialized training for their type of aircraft, such as using **flight simulators** that look and act like the planes they are learning to fly.

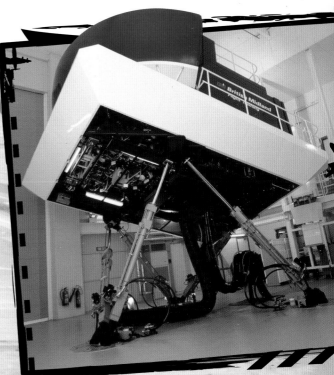

➤ Flight simulators help pilots learn how to fly safely.

◄ Aircraft carriers provide runways on which military planes can land at sea.

AIRCRAFT CARRIERS

Military airplanes are sometimes needed in a war zone far from their home country. The government will usually get permission from another nation to build an air base on their land. However, it is often quicker and easier to bring the planes to the other country by sea, on a giant aircraft carrier. An aircraft carrier is a boat that has a flight deck with runways for the planes. In good weather, two airplanes can be launched and one can land every 37 seconds.

Moving planes around

While some aeroplanes are stored on the flight deck, most are kept three levels down, on the hangar deck. Lifts strong enough to hold two fighter jets at once carry the planes between the decks. When the aeroplanes are not being used, they are strapped down so the movement of the ship on the ocean will not damage them.

▲ These two aeroplanes are being lifted from the hangar deck to the flight deck by a super-strong lift.

Arresting wires
wires on which a jet plane's tailhook catches to stop the plane

Jet engine shop
the ship's planes can be repaired on board

Propellers
these move the ship through the water. Each one weighs about 30 tonnes

Radar
tells crew members where jets and other ships are

FACT!
The American Nimitz Class aircraft carrier is the largest warship ever built. It has a crew of 6000.

Hangar deck
where the planes are stored when they are not flying

Aircraft lifts
Four of these lifts carry planes between the hangar deck and the flight deck

PUBLIC-USE AIRPORTS

Most large airports have so many **commercial flights** that they cannot allow small planes to take off and land on their runways. Airfields for public use are smaller airports that provide runways and services for smaller planes, which may be owned by an individual or small company rather than a large airline or the military. A public-use airport often has only one runway, a small **refuelling station**, and an airplane maintenance center. However, it might also have a flight school, **charter airlines**, and a public viewing area.

▲ The Stellenbosch Airfield in South Africa is a public-use airport.

Lightweight aircraft, ➤ such as this one at Crystal River airport in Florida, are tied down at three main points to keep them in position.

RAMP IT UP

While some planes at public-use airports are stored inside hangars, many are kept outdoors in an airplane parking area called a ramp. The ramp is a paved surface or a grassy field near the hangars and airport buildings. The planes' wings and tails are strapped to tie-downs so they are not blown over by heavy winds.

Safety first

Most small airfields do not have a full-time air traffic control tower to give the pilots information about the weather, where they should land, and where to drive the plane once they are on the ground. Instead, signs and markings on the runway and taxiway tell the pilot where to go. Runway lights that can be controlled by the pilot's radio and a bright rotating **beacon** help guide the plane to the airport at night.

▲ A brightly colored wind sock near the runway shows the pilot in which direction and how hard the wind is blowing.

AIRPARKS

Some people who have their own planes build their houses in an area near a private runway so that they can fly their planes whenever they want. These areas are called airparks. The roads at an airpark are often very wide so that they can connect directly to the airport runway. After landing, the pilot can **taxi** the plane straight home! Some planes are kept at tie-downs on parking ramps near the runway. Airparks are growing more common, especially in vacation spots.

◀ An airplane driving down the street is a common sight in a residential airpark.

Park it

Many houses in an airpark community have garages that are like small airplane hangars. These garages are wide enough for a small plane and have large doors that flip up to let the plane in or out. The pilot uses a towrope attached to the front wheel to pull the plane out of the garage, then hops in and drives to the runway. It is just like having a car with wings!

▼ This house has a garage big enough for the owner's private plane.

N9070V

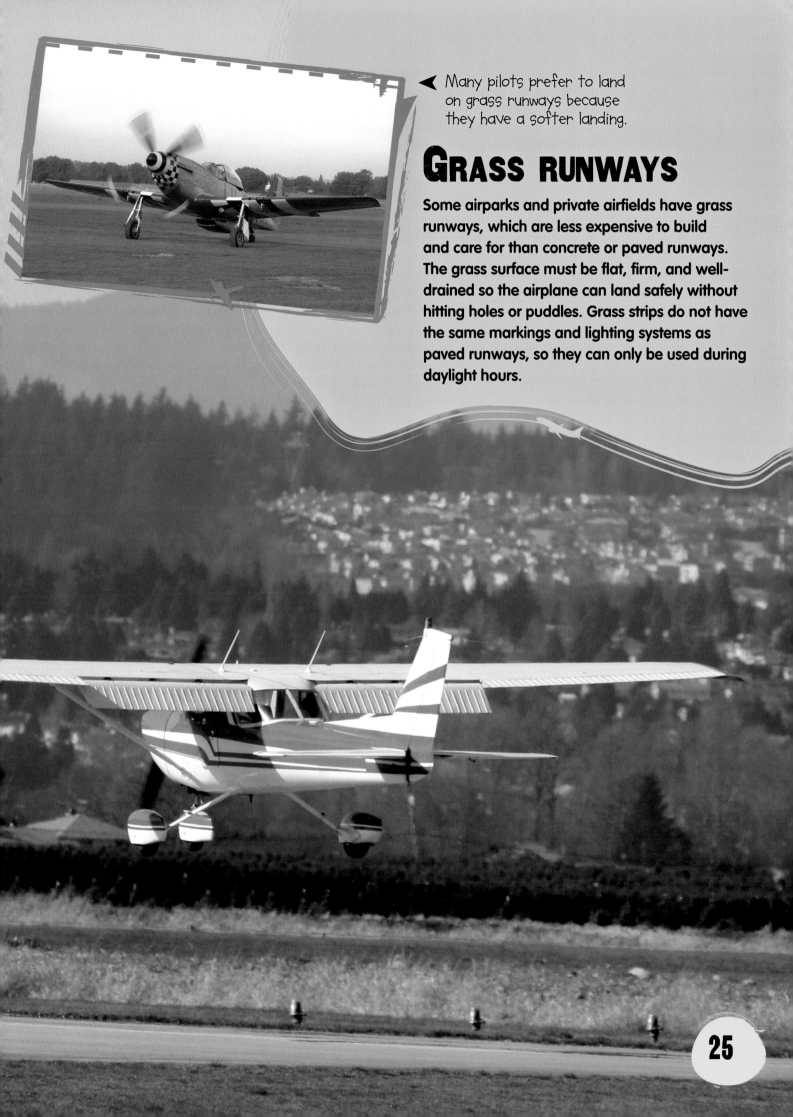

◀ Many pilots prefer to land on grass runways because they have a softer landing.

GRASS RUNWAYS

Some airparks and private airfields have grass runways, which are less expensive to build and care for than concrete or paved runways. The grass surface must be flat, firm, and well-drained so the airplane can land safely without hitting holes or puddles. Grass strips do not have the same markings and lighting systems as paved runways, so they can only be used during daylight hours.

SEAPLANE BASES

Seaplanes are airplanes that can land on the water. Most seaplanes have two floats called pontoons that hang below the body of the plane and allow it to land without sinking. Seaplanes are often used in remote, isolated areas where the land is too hilly for a flat runway. A seaplane base may be a sandy beach where the planes can be pulled near the shore, or it may have a series of docks, a fuelling station, a maintenance area, and a terminal, just like a normal airport.

▼ This busy seaplane base has many parking docks, a fuelling station, and a terminal for passengers.

A seaplane glides ► across the water on its pontoons as it lands.

No waves

A seaplane can only take off or land when the water is very calm. Most seaplane bases are located on lakes or rivers that are protected from strong winds by trees and hills. These areas of water do not have many waves, so the planes can land smoothly.

WHEELS AND FLOATS

Many seaplanes can take off and land both on water and on land. These amphibious planes have wheels that extend from their floats for landing on paved runways. In bad weather, when the waves are too rough for a safe water landing, these planes can fly to a nearby airport.

◄ Seaplanes are often used to take vacationers on short journeys between nearby islands.

FACT!

The Lake Hood Seaplane Base in Alaska is the busiest in the world, with nearly 200 flights per day.

HELIPORTS

A heliport is a small airport for helicopters. Helicopters do not need runways and can land on most flat, firm surfaces, but a heliport usually has several landing pads. The outline of the landing area is always marked and the center is usually painted with a giant letter H in a circle. Heliports may also have a small terminal, hangar space, lights, and a wind indicator. Some heliports are used mainly for emergency services, while others are run as a business.

➤ The helicopter has landed at a heliport.

TAKING OFF

A helicopter works a bit like an electric fan. Four blades are connected to a central rotor that spins them around very quickly. As air is pushed down by the blades, the helicopter is lifted into the air. The smaller rotor and blades on the tail prevent the helicopter from spinning in circles. The rotors can be adjusted to make the helicopter fly up or down or turn in either direction.

◄ Helicopter blades push air down to lift the aircraft off the ground.

Night lights

Many helicopter landing areas are used at night and require special lighting. **Floodlights** are pointed toward the ground to light up the landing pad. A line of yellow lights marks the best approach and departure path, while more yellow lights outline the landing area. Red lights mark obstacles near the landing area.

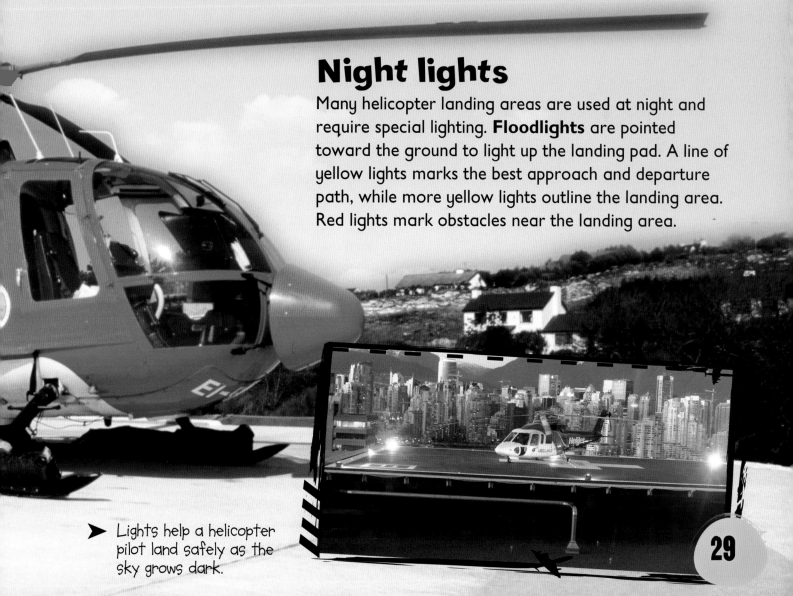

➤ Lights help a helicopter pilot land safely as the sky grows dark.

HELIPADS

A helicopter is useful because it can take off and land in small areas that do not have enough room for an airplane runway. Helicopters also save on travel time because they are faster than cars or boats. Helipads are landing pads, often made from concrete, that give helicopters a stable, well-marked place to land. Some lighthouses off the coast of Britain have helipads on top, allowing repair workers to get to them more easily. Oil rigs also use helicopters to bring workers to and from the coast.

➤ Many skyscrapers, such as the Burj Al Arab in Dubai, have helipads for business travelers.

On top of the city

Some skyscrapers have private helipads on their roofs, so business people can avoid heavy city traffic on their way to important meetings. Some hospitals also have helipads on their roofs so that badly injured patients can be taken to hospital more quickly. In small villages, far away from the main hospitals, helicopters can pick up emergency patients and take them to the nearest hospital for treatment.

ON THE SEA

Many ships, such as aircraft carriers and oil tankers, have a helipad onboard. This is so the ships do not have to head back to port every time people or supplies are transferred between land and the ship — helicopters can bring any visitors and supplies to them.

▲ Some luxury yachts have a flat platform for a helicopter to land on.

READING & BATES

RB

JIM CUNNINGHAM

▲ Helipads allow helicopters to land in areas with no flat, solid land, such as an oil rig out at sea.

SPACEPORTS

Rockets and space shuttles do not take off down a runway, like airplanes. They must launch straight up into the air with enough force to escape Earth's gravity. A **spaceport** has a concrete launch pad that can withstand the high heat of a rocket's burning fuel during its launch. Spacecraft are not able to taxi around the spaceport like a plane, either. The **NASA** space agency uses a giant **crawler machine** to slowly carry the space shuttle from the vehicle assembly building to the **launch pad**, a journey of 4 miles (6.5 kilometers).

The Space Shuttle ➤ Discovery travels to the launch pad.

FACT!

The runway at NASA's Kennedy Space Center in Florida is more than 14,764 feet (4,500 meters) long, about 4,920 feet (1,500 meters) longer than an average airport runway.

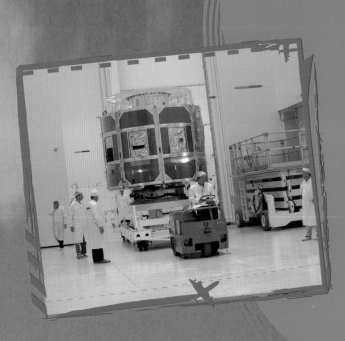

Satellites

Most spacecraft carry payloads such as satellites, scientific experiments, or supplies into space. These payloads must be kept very clean so that they do not break down while in space. The rooms in the satellite preparation area are kept sterile and workers must wear covers over their clothes, shoes, and hair to prevent tiny pieces of dirt from contaminating the satellites.

◀ Scientists at Europe's spaceport in French Guiana wear lab coats and protective gear to keep this satellite clean.

Coming home

The space shuttle is designed to land on **retractable** wheels, like a normal airplane. However, when it touches down on the runway, it is moving so fast from reentering Earth's **atmosphere** that it has to eject a parachute to help slow it down. If bad weather prevents the astronauts from landing at Kennedy Space Center, they have the option of landing at NASA spaceports in Texas or California. When this happens, a 747 airplane, called the Shuttle Carrier Aircraft, flies the shuttle back to Florida. It has to stop for fuel several times along the way.

➤ The space shuttle lands on a runway like a normal airplane, but needs a drag chute to help it to slow down.

GLOSSARY

air traffic controller A person who tells pilots along which routes and at what heights they should fly their planes

amphibious Something that can travel both on land and in water

arresting wires Thick, strong metal ropes that stop a jet plane's forward movement

atmosphere The gases surrounding the Earth

barcode A label with a pattern of lines that gives a computer information about an object

beacon A bright light

cargo Goods carried by an airplane, ship, or train

catapult A device that helps a fighter jet gain a lot of speed over a short distance

charter airlines Companies that are hired to provide air travel for a group of passengers

check in When passengers show their tickets to an airline agent, hand over the bags they want to go into the hold, and are assigned their seats for the flight

civilian Something that is used by everyday people, not the military

commercial flights Flights provided by an airline company that makes money by charging passengers to travel

confiscated Taken away

connections When passengers stop at an airport along the way to their destination to change aircraft

contaminating Making something unusable by allowing a harmful substance to touch it

conveyor belt A moving belt that takes luggage from one place to another

courier companies Businesses that transport and deliver packages

crawler machine A vehicle with caterpillar tracks instead of wheels that takes the Space Shuttle to the launch pad

destination The place to which a person is traveling

flight deck The top deck of an aircraft carrier, where planes land and take off

flight number A number used to identify a plane and the route it is taking

flight simulator A machine that recreates the sights, sounds, and feel of flying a plane

floodlights Lamps that shine light over a wide area during poor light or at night

gates Numbered exits where passengers leave the terminal to board their airplanes

ground crew People who look after the airplanes when they are on the ground and get them ready to fly

hangar Huge buildings where airplanes are stored or taken to be repaired

helipads Take off and landing areas for helicopters

hold The area in a plane where luggage and cargo are kept

launch pad The platform from which a spacecraft is launched

metal detector A device used to test for metals

NASA The National Aeronautics and Space Administration—the space agency

nose The front tip of an airplane

payloads Cargo or instruments carried into space by a space shuttle

radar A machine that uses radio waves to track the locations of aircraft

refuelling station An area where fuel is pumped into the planes

regional airport An airport that does not have flights to other countries

retractable Able to be pulled back in

rotor The part of a helicopter that spins the blades

runways A long track, often paved, on which planes take off and land

scan Read with a device to send data to a computer

security screening The process through which passengers are checked to make sure they are allowed on the plane

spaceport An airport for launching spacecraft

sterile Very clean, free of germs

suspension bridge A bridge that is supported by large metal ropes, which are connected to towers

tailhook A curved device on the back of a fighter jet that hooks onto the arresting wires on an aircraft carrier

taxi To drive an airplane along the ground at a low speed

taxiways Tracks that pilots drive along to get their planes from the terminal to the runway, or vice versa

terminal The building at an airport in which passengers buy tickets, check their luggage, and board the planes

test flight A trip made in a new type of airplane to make sure it is safe and ready to be used

tie-downs Devices used to attach a small plane to the ramp so that the wind will not move it or flip it over

touchdown The moment when a plane first touches the ground on landing

transfer point An airport where travelers switch from one plane to another while making a connection

FIND OUT MORE

Learn how Hong Kong International Airport was built:
http://dsc.discovery.com/convergence/engineering/airport/interactive/interactive.html

Find more information about how aircraft carriers work:
http://www.science.howstuffworks.com/aircraft-carrier.htm

Watch the air traffic at Newark International Airport:
http://www4.passur.com/ewr.html

Read about how the space shuttle is prepared for launch:
http://www.nasa.gov/audience/forkids/artsstories/AS_Steps_to_Countdown.html

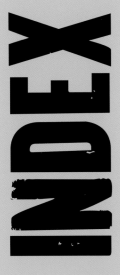

INDEX